SUNDAY DINNER
AT THE FARM

poems by

Nancy Corson Carter

Finishing Line Press
Georgetown, Kentucky

SUNDAY DINNER AT THE FARM

Copyright © 2016 by Nancy Corson Carter
ISBN 978-1-944899-68-4 First Edition
All rights reserved under International and Pan-American Copyright Conventions.
No part of this book may be reproduced in any manner whatsoever without written permission from the publisher, except in the case of brief quotations embodied in critical articles and reviews.

ACKNOWLEDGMENTS

My grateful acknowledgment to the following publications in which some of the poems in this collection first appeared: Anima ("Evocation"); Yet Another Small Magazine ("For Grammy On Her 90th Birthday" and "Katie"); limited edition calligraphic print collaboration with Denys Taipale, "Apple Basket"; Pudding Magazine: The International Journal of Applied Poetry ("Pickled Beets and Hard-Boiled Eggs," "Sunday Dinner," and "A Childhood Reminiscence"); Bellowing Ark ("Apple Basket," "Five-Toe Exercise," "My Grandmother's Piano," "Daddy," "A Return" "Otto Romaine Corson," and "Thirteenth Quilt: White on White").

The cover piggies photo and the author portrait are by Howard Carter. The photo of Grammy Corson at the piano and the one of her holding up the onion from her garden are by Nancy Corson Carter. The others are from the Corson family collection.

Publisher: Leah Maines

Editor: Christen Kincaid

Cover Art: Howard Carter

Author Photo: Howard Carter

Cover Design: Elizabeth Maines

Printed in the USA on acid-free paper.
Order online: www.finishinglinepress.com
        also available on amazon.com

        Author inquiries and mail orders:
            Finishing Line Press
             P. O. Box 1626
        Georgetown, Kentucky 40324
               U. S. A.

Table of Contents

Evocation 1

Sunday Dinner 2

Otto Romaine Corson 4

Grammy and Aunt Pauline on Wash Day, c. 1925 6

A Childhood Reminiscence 7

Daddy 9

Family Bible 11

Katie 13

Golden 14

Apple Basket 15

Eve's Gift of Applesauce 16

Pickled Beets and Hard-Boiled Eggs 18

Five-Toe Exercise 20

Winter Night Ride 21

13th Quilt: White on White 22

Cave Mother 23

For Grammy on Her 90th Birthday 24

My Grandmother's Piano 26

Seeing the Farm through a Glass Darkly 27

A Grade School Excursion into Pennsylvania Autumn 28

A Return 30

*To my grandparents Otto and Cora Alice Corson,
to my parents, Harvey and Dorothy Corson, and
to all who have gathered around this table.*

"One eats in holiness and the table becomes an altar."
—Martin Buber

EVOCATION

In the cold bedroom
    I often stop
    on errands to fetch jam
    from the attic storage place.

Your black dress, Grandma,
    hangs on the closet door:
    prim crepe, jet-beaded collar,
    your familiar smell.

In the dining room below:
    winter woodstove cooking,
    steamy windows,
    jovial aunts and uncles.

On the dark-stained dresser:
    your hairpins and brooches
    in flower-painted dishes,
    Grandpa's boxes of mints and salves.

Your worn brass bed:
    under its quilted curves lie
    ghosts of embraces.

I am afraid the stiff couple
    in the marriage portrait
    will laugh or cry "Thief!"

Afraid the stuffed hawk
    will sweep from the guest room
    and pierce my eyes.

Trying to avoid the boards that creak,
    I stand on the braided stocking rug
    and see in your ancient mirror:
    I am no longer a child.

SUNDAY DINNER

In the dark-paneled room,
the centered table's linen
framed bowls and platters
displaying Grammy's art:

Jellies, pickles, and beets;
tomatoes, beans, coleslaw,
sweet corn, and fresh bread
(desserts hidden for later).

Mouths watering, we welcomed
my cousin's quick blessing:
"Good God, let's eat;
please pass the meat!"

In a print on one wall
the Good Shepherd assented;
in a photo beside it,
President Eisenhower grinned.

Grandpap spilled coffee
into his saucer to cool;
he'd scoop peas on his knife
till our kidding stopped him.

In hunting season we hoped
for ring-necked pheasant—
a treat roasted with sherry—
but we watched for shot pellets!

Our Sunday ritual outlasted
stacks of local bank calendars;
then Grandpap died and
everything changed.

OTTO ROMAINE CORSON

In the mirror I see my grandpap's nose,
That bumpy germanic legacy.
Daddy once said to me in comradely pity
"You and I both inherited it."

I wish I'd had his bright blue eyes instead;
I wished, then, I was my father's son,
His grandson, privy to menfolks' secrets of
Crop yields and sales, tractors, and livestock.

I did things a granddaughter might
To win his praise: helped Grammy fix meals,
Pulled weeds by the barn, showed him good grades,
And tried to be truthful.

He reigned as patriarch at Sunday dinner,
Telling jokes, lambasting politicians,
Insisting we try some smierkäse, scrapple,
Or maybe cheddar he'd bought wholesale
On his weekly city market trip.

In the family album, he looks stern and large.
His clothes look rough, unstarched, worn;
He wears suspenders because of hernias;
A felt fedora hides his bald pate.

From the buffet behind his chair
I took out stereoscope cards
For my crossed-eye exercises;
With effort, I saw two images
Merged in 3-D illusion.

Grammy called him "Ottie."
When he smiled at her
His gruffness disappeared.
Though age now blurs my focus
That's the image I hold dearest.

GRAMMY AND AUNT PAULINE ON WASH DAY, c. 1925

*"There is nothing, nothing, nothing,
that two women cannot do before noon."*
    —*Jean Giraudoux, "The Madwoman of Chaillot"*

Although frost still threatens,
a few flowers poke up;
maybe an early robin calls.
The first wash loads steamed
in the tub like butchering scald;
with luck the sheets won't
freeze hard on the lines.

They've pumped cistern water,
boiled it in great pots on
the cast iron woodstove.
There's been stirring, rinsing,
wringing, and hanging of
laundry for seven.
Tomorrow is ironing day.

Though I doubt they've read them,
they've met the women's magazines'
standards for "cleanliness,
cheerfulness, and efficiency" in this,
"the homemaker's most arduous task."

You might think them carefree unless
you counted other chores still waiting
or felt their hands roughened by
washboards and lye soap.

Still, their smiles are genuine.
Their embracing arms
form a proud yoke of women's
work done well, with love.

A CHILDHOOD REMINISCENCE

Grandpap said the preacher was a liar
so he refused to enter the Baptist church
only 500 yards down the hill from his farm.
I figured if he said so, it must be true.

Grammy, however, tried to make peace,
wore a cross around her neck, and
made bread for communion; in adult class
she kept perfect attendance.

On hot summer afternoon visits,
tired of kick-the-can and chasing cats,
we cousins sneaked into the one-room church,
closed the doors, and snooped around.

We played baptizing in the empty font,
preaching from the fat pulpit Bible.
When we mimed a collection, I wondered:
did the preacher lie to keep the money?

Over the altar, a large painting of
Jesus in a garish Gethsemane—
how could He look so peaceful
kneeling to pray among thorns?

In the hard, right-angled pews
we cooled ourselves with
Jesus Loves You fans, provided
Courtesy of Stein's Ford Garage.

Bored and restless, we returned to fresh air,
one more game before supper.
Unlike church rules, our rules were clear:
"Last one to the pump is IT!"

DADDY

He went to war
six weeks after I was born.
Three years later,
an Army wool-coat giant
rose from the stairs to
our second floor porch.
I hid behind Mama, asked
"Who's that man?"

Then Daddy and Mama
put away the war years
like a book of bad dreams;
Daddy intended to
make up for lost time.

Life roared into action like
Army trucks he bought
to haul combines and tractors
for the new family business.

He knew things about land,
animals, people, and guns,
about money and machines,
that made the world around him
feel large and safe.

You'd want to have Daddy along
if your vehicle stalled,
if you ran out of food,
if you needed honest work done,
or straight words said.

He made a Norman Rockwell
portrait with his girls
(Mama and then *four* daughters)
in tow for Friday night out—
Village Tea Room sticky buns,
a little shopping, and, with luck,
a John Wayne film at the Rialto.

From his days as spelling bee
champ at country school,
he taught us hard words
like "phlegm," "ukulele,"
"Czechoslovakia," and "depot."
I read his Zane Grey novels and
The Young Carthaginian.

Because he didn't like to handwrite
(maybe tiny tremors
presaged his Parkinson's),
I treasure his few postcards
and his note in a dictionary
he and Mama gave me:
"Nancy—make good use of this book."

FAMILY BIBLE

Between the two Testaments
of the big King James
a few foxed pages
bear the "Family Register."

Grammy's neat
Palmer Method cursive
records five live births:
two daughters and three sons.

Miscarriages fall away
between the lines;
a stillborn is listed
as "Baby C."

Smudged birth date numbers
betray one daughter's pride:
she never told her husband
she was older than he was.

Noted: five marriages,
a sprinkling of baptisms,
only one son's son to
carry on the family name.

In those days divorce
was rare and shameful;
you can feel the weight
of crossing one pair out.

Nineteen great-grandchildren,
and at least three great-greats
born after Grammy died
or she'd have entered their names.

The Bible's now an artifact
of a family dispersed,
its records pressed and faded
like an old corsage.

KATIE

My childhood memory fixed you
        as old, complaining, piteous,
An orphan servant maid
Telling frightful stories of
        blacksnakes coiling on cellar shelves,
        geese attacking in the pasture.
Your waist-length grey hair
        was your singular vanity.

That crazy-quilt pillow you made as a girl:
The prettiest thing on Grammy's sofa.
What dreams did you dream
        as you fancifully stitched
        those satins and velvets?

Surely not living alone in a tiny cubicle,
        bed and bureau squeezed between
        cornflake boxes and lard cans
        behind my grandparents' bedroom.

Surely not the bunioned feet and cataracts,
Coarse black dress and hand-me-down
        coat for church,
Daily hobbling from milking to egg-gathering,
In fly-stinging summers, wind-shrilling winters.

Years after you are gone and I am grown,
I remember that pillow—
One bright piece in your patchwork life.

GOLDEN

We pick buckets of finger-staining dandelions;
Grammy transforms them into wine.

*

A beeswax, onionskins, and vinegar recipe
Makes old-fashioned ochre Easter eggs.

*

We vie for warm bronzy crusts of
Fresh round loaves cut in snowy slabs.

*

Burnished walnuts adorn hard white
Sugar glaze on lard-shortened cake.

*

Sweet corn dries in wood-warmed oven
Into nuggets preserved for family feasts.

*

Yellow snaps boiled and served hot with butter—
If there's more in the garden, we'll take some home.

*

Copper kettles simmer for three autumn days,
Yield clove-dark apple butter, inimitably fine.

*

Spicewood tea in blue Pyrex cups:
Spring tonic from still-bare woods.

*

Buttercups we picked out back by the silo
Glow on the table in a cut glass vase.

*

Sun-spackled oilcloth surrounds my page:
I keep on writing 'til it's time to eat.

APPLE BASKET

for my father, who knew and loved apples

Once these thin ribs encircled
Winesap, Jonathan, Delicious,
Baldwin, McIntosh, Rome Beauty—
All these varieties and more:

Sheepnose, Ben Davis, and Russet.
These gently swelling alveoli
Pulsed the breath of the sky
Into prize orchard fruits.

Pickers' hands and weathering
Stained the light staves dark,
Rusted the handles,
Bent and mildewed the wood.

Sweet hay and apple esters
Scent the shed's cool air;
The basket's frail shell
Resembles a chalice.

This humble relic
Calls forth sorrow and hope;
The old orchard's a ghost,
But new apples ripen.

EVE'S GIFT OF APPLESAUCE

We cut and peeled for hours
at apple harvest time.
When I was bored, I sliced
bruised ones crosswise to see
five-seed stars gleam.

Grammy tackled
the worst apples first,
a thrifty, slow approach;
I rummaged, instead,
for the biggest and nicest
so I could do *more, faster.*

We used mostly windfalls
(spared by deer and rabbits),
but Pollies were Grammy's choice,
Yellow Transparents, Mama's.

I'll name mine *Dianas*
for that Ephesian goddess
of many ample breasts.
Their milky juice spills
remembrance of

Sieving hot boiled apples,
stirring cinnamon sugar
into sweet steamy clouds.

From the crockery cauldron,
our green Fiestaware bowl,
I call up apple-wise women
in a line I trace to Eve . . .

Eve! her infamous tasting
must have led to imagining
the incomparable sauce,
its enticing perfume.
Surely she's the mother of
this apple-loving art!

**PICKLED BEETS
AND HARD-BOILED EGGS**

As the beet root
conceals its alchemy
of changing pallid soil
into deep carmine,
the dyed eggs,
firm and slippery,
withhold their secrets
until the knife
slices oxblood skin
clean through,
and two gold circles
flash soft
blind light.

FIVE-TOE EXERCISE

This little piggy went to market . . .
      Grandpap took him to Williamsport,
      Exchanged him
           for a truckload of dry goods.

This little piggy stayed home . . .
      I swatted seven flies with
           one blow above her trough;
      Being illiterate, she was not impressed.

This little piggy had roast beef . . .
      Fibber! We fed him kitchen slops
      Besides mash and dry corn
      While we dreamed of porkchops.

This little piggy had none . . .
      She was slim enough to squeeze out
      For one last fling in clover
      Before Grandpap pig-proofed
           the pen forever.

This little piggy cried "Wee, wee, wee"
           all the way home . . .
      But I consoled him with happy endings
      Like Wilbur's in *Charlotte's Web*,
      And he happily played carefree 'til bedtime.

WINTER NIGHT RIDE

Over snowy roads home,
Daddy drives, Mother's beside him;
In the backseat, kids drowse
To the motor's steady hum.

My breath etches the window
With a reverie of summer past;
Crystals form a shape that
Surprised me at the brook:

Great Blue Heron—
Dagger bill, plumed head,
Slate blue caped body—
A gallant messenger for

A young girl dreaming
Of her fairytale prince
In some bright future
Secretly beckoning.

I watch wide-fanned wings
Graze an astonished moon;
They glide past the hill crest
Then fade into sky sea.

Car wheels grind gravel
In our driveway tracks.

THIRTEENTH QUILT: WHITE ON WHITE

This thirteen's lucky, I just know it:
White on white for our wedding,
My hope chest's prize quilt.

My cornsilk fine thread's almost
Baler-twine strong; the batting's
As soft as my kitten's furry belly.

My stitches track as evenly as
quail prints on snow, as smoothly
As flour on well-kneaded bread.

White on white's the smell of roses,
It's a lark's first spring song;
It's my glad "Yes!" to your "Marry me?"

White on white's summer sun flare,
Buckwheat blossoms at twilight;
It's fresh-washed linen snapping in the wind.

White on white's autumn fog,
The lacy first frost;
It's our rising breath in morning chill.

White on white's the drift of snow,
Deer tails flicking out of sight;
It's sugar and flour for Christmas cakes.

Dreaming of us, I retrace old patterns
Of flowers, of fruits, and, surely the best:
Two white doves snuggled close in their nest.

CAVE MOTHER

From the Grandparent Farm
High on the hill
Snow melt and wash water
Body wastes and rain
Pigslops and pest sprays
Trickle down, trickle down

Past grubs and beetles
Past depths of the plow;
Matted hair roots filter
Pain and pleasure's remains.
Receptive earth distills all.

This liquor fattens
The toothless mother;
Stuporous snores rise
From her cave mouth below.

She bloats the hill, her
Great stomach, high in the air;
Her belches brings storms,
Her farts, nightmares.

Webs tickle our faces
As we peek over her
Grass-furred gums;
Her cool, loamy breath
Tempts us to come closer.
We stand here shivering,
Half hoping she'll speak.

FOR GRAMMY ON HER 90TH BIRTHDAY

Cora Alice Smith Corson:
Our daughter's second name is Alice, too;
I will remember you to her.
Your letters used to say
"I wish you were here to have supper with me,"
And I would taste delights like fresh-made
Apple butter, rhubarb or shoofly pie,
Perhaps a little dandelion wine.

Stern rock-ridden Pennsylvania hill soil
Distilled your spirit into sweetest spring water.
I see your freckled workworn hands
Husking, hoeing, skinning, milking,
Clapping in delight, reaching to comfort,
Playing hymns on your piano
Arrayed with family photos.

After Grandpap's death, the farm sold,
You moved to town alone;
You never lost the simple gift
Of sharing all you had.
Behind the ample dining table,
Your ferns and rocker rested side by side;
Each home you made breathed peace.

Now you shine on a mountain high above us,
Your mind broken by age's holy madness;
You do not know our faces
Though we see ourselves in yours.

If only I could say
"Grammy, come have supper with us tonight,"
And you'd be here!

MY GRANDMOTHER'S PIANO

Grammy loved to play
"Sweet Hour of Prayer"
from the Baptist hymnal
on the black upright.

I practiced that hymn
until I could play it too;
even Daddy would
sometimes sing along.

In that chilly front parlor
we kids played "Chopsticks"
so raucously the grown-ups
closed the keyboard lid.

On the round piano stool
we made ourselves dizzy,
spinning and spinning 'til
we fell down, laughing.

Grammy would sing solo
in her sweet reedy voice
if my Mom accompanied her
with "How Great Thou Art."

Now I imagine Grammy
at a concert grand;
she plays "Morning Has Broken"
like there is no tomorrow.

SEEING THE FARM THROUGH A GLASS DARKLY

Behind the tar-papered henhouse
In the farm's back edges,
We imagine snakes and mad dogs
As we wade through high grass.

Rhubarb and currants huddle
Outside the garden's pale;
If you hide here for kick-the-can,
You'll never get home free.

Over the hill, at the Birketts'
Lurk a bull and nasty geese.
Barbed wire prickles round
Their mucky pasture.

My lonesome memories
Resemble funnel clouds:
The oily green air
Whirls roaring disaster.

When it all settles out,
There's no trace of the farm—
Its few survivors
Are far away, scattered.

On my desk is a rose
Like the ones Grammy grew;
Her faith bloomed like her garden,
A reminder of the light.

A GRADE SCHOOL EXCURSION INTO PENNSYLVANIA AUTUMN

Our chunky yellow school bus
magically dissolves
into blurs and billows
of yellow leaves in fog.

We might be Thumbelinas
inside glowing daffodils
or saffron-silked Chinese
afloat a Yellow River.

Outlines wobble past of
the church where Brownies meet,
my piano teacher's cottage,
the Ritz Theatre on Main.

Gauzy air on Water Street
veils that pretty Joanna's house;
further on, the swimming hole's
sunk in a fog bank.

Clarkstown bridge planking
clatters by beneath us;
hedgerows of sumac and
asters brush our windows.

There's a mill with a creaky
still-turning waterwheel,
a farm where my Dad sold
an Allis-Chalmers tractor.

Maple leaves drift down
into earth-scented quilts;
we could ride forever
in this peaceable kingdom.

A RETURN

I

High on the hill above the Farm
I stood in snow, sled rope held tight;
I knew if I dared, I could fly.

A sound beyond the drifted fields
Held me hovering,
Tempted but afraid to yield.

Now this sound recurs;
In a dream I fly back . . .

Sled with me down the alabaster track
Past the orchard and garden,
The yard wall and garage;
Curve left by the churchyard fence,
Past the chapel, the bronzed oak grove.

This time with extra weight—
Daddy's on the bottom!—
We'll make it down the last stretch
To the paved highway.

II

Flying back through doors of seasons,
I go to make this gathering.
Do you remember picking
      mayapples by the stream,
      moss rose in the cemetery,
      wintergreen berries among pine roots?

III

We float about the house;
We do not wake the new people;
They cannot see what we are here to find:
In the living room, the plaster Diana with hounds,
The funeral portrait of Grandpap's favorite sister,
The furnace grating that ballooned our skirts,
That nasty rocker that pinched our fingers;
In the attic, sleigh bells on nails,
Christmas ornaments in boxes,
Jelly jars on the steps;

In the cellar, egg cartons on cool earth floor,
A whole stalk of bananas from the city market,
A tin of sugar cookies on the ledge by the door;

In the kitchen, Grandpap's rocker by the woodstove,
Grammy's babytears and aloe on the window sill;
In the drawer beneath the clock shelf, the clippers
Daddy used to shave Grandpap's head.

IV

Hush, there are others here.
Grandpap walks from the barn to his garage
Where row on row the nail kegs, bolt boxes, tools
Line walls beside the Dodge pickup.

Look through the cobwebbed windows;
Grammy could be just around the corner,
Bent-shouldered, faithful about chores.

Run, we might catch her,
Then she'll let us go once more
Into that rustling, feather-dusty coop
To find warm brown eggs.

V

Around by the woodshed
Grammy's blue morning glories
Climb taut yellow twine.
Pussywillows sprout from this crevice each spring:
Between milk house and porch we can just squeeze in,
a really good place for hide-and-go-seek.
In the garden, see cockscomb and yarrow by the path,
Dahlias, Grammy's prizes, heavy-headed in the corner;
Near the gate, peonies, japonica, and Rose of Sharon.

Her hollyhocks and tiger lilies
Brighten grey chimney stones;
Each familiar flower's roots go deep.

VI

Out on those stony hills, that recalcitrant soil,
I stand in buzzing summer, waist-deep in wheat;
Dust plumes from a lone Sunday car.

The ghost of a white horse gallops toward me;
It seems like a friend—I'm not afraid.
I come to meet it, let it nuzzle my hand.

VII

Golden antlers appeared by the woods;
We took them back to protect the house.
We painted the gables with milk and honey;
For so many years this was our refuge.

And so it remains:
I stand again on the truck-greasing platform
In autumn chill, wearing that old blue
Cotton sweater with the stretched-out neck;

I shout across the cemetery
To the asbestos-shingled church:
"I remember! I remember!"

And echoes return
From this hallowed bowl of hills.

This writing is based upon a family ritual my father began when he returned home after serving in the US Army in World War II. Each Sunday he drove Mother, my sisters, and me to visit his parents' farm near Muncy in central Pennsylvania. This tradition lasted until Grandpap died in 1957 and Grammy moved to town.

Late one night many years later, I traveled in my imagination back to the grandparent farm. As I walked about the house and land, I began to map what I call a geography of the heart in poems and prose.

I believe that all of us construct our own unique maps of places we've lived in or visited (or imagined), places that we will always recall with love. These maps often appear unexpectedly when some sight—like the photos I've included—or sound or smell unfolds them again.

Once I saw the front room (usually unheated) of that farmhouse alive with the busyness of a quilting bee. I send such convivial energy to all who read and imagine along with me. May my "patchwording" evoke sensations for you of warmth and beauty that last beyond loss.